"Here's to my body, my first home,
my only country,
the miracle I get to inhabit. Mine.
Every day, mine."

SAFIA ELHILLO

Design by Diane Shaw

ISBN: 978-1-4197-3828-9

Text © 2019 Fariha Róisín
Illustrations © 2019 Monica Ramos

Cover © 2019 Abrams

Printed and bound in China
10 9 8 7 6 5 4 3

Abrams Noterie products are available at special discounts when purchased in quantity
for premiums and promotions as well as fundraising or educational use. Special editions
can also be created to specification. For details, contact specialsales@abramsbooks.com
or the address below.

Abrams Noterie® is a registered trademark of Harry N. Abrams, Inc.

ABRAMS The Art of Books
195 Broadway, New York, NY 10007
abramsbooks.com

MIX
Paper from
responsible sources
FSC™ C144853

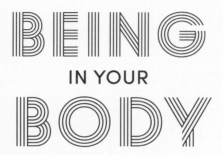

BEING
IN YOUR
BODY

A Journal for Self-Love
and Body Positivity

FARIHA RÓISÍN

Illustrations by Monica Ramos

ABRAMS NOTERIE, NEW YORK

WHY MUST YOU LIKE YOURSELF IN HINDSIGHT?

WHAT IF YOU LIKED YOURSELF TODAY?

This journal intends to instigate breakthroughs in our ideas of our bodies, our selves, and all that confines us. It asks us to consider what our lives would be like without that nagging, negative inner monologue about our bodies. It offers an opportunity to explore that possibility, while still being honest about our insecurities and unpacking the bromides we've been taught by society. This is a space for women, femmes, nonbinary folks, or anyone who needs to be reminded that who they are, exactly as they are, is valuable.

We've all been fed negative ideas about what makes a body worthy of existence, but I want to remind you that the only valid response to your body is your own. Yes, that may not always be positive, but I want this journal to be a guide to the possibility of liking oneself. Self-love is the goal, but it's not really the destination. Self-love is an up-and-down process, and that's OK.

But, let's be clear about the concepts. "Self-love" is looking in the mirror and deciding that we are beautiful and worthy of good treatment, despite the negative messaging we receive about our bodies. "Body positivity" is actively fighting against those standards by acknowledging the fact that some people move through the world with challenges and others enjoy privileges, simply based on the bodies that they occupy.

Though this journal is more about doing the work of self-love than body positivity, the two are intertwined, especially when it comes to the process of unlearning negative messaging. In order to practice true self-love, we have to understand that the opposite (self-hatred) comes from oppressive social forces that ultimately affect everyone, even the seemingly privileged. The struggle to love oneself is not a problem that we've each individually invented; it is ingrained in us by social conditions that prioritize a specific kind of body. But the truth is, you will only be convinced that your body is adequate, worthy, and beautiful if you can see all bodies this way.

HERE ARE SOME TERMS TO THINK ABOUT:

Ableism: Society has created standards of living that benefit and prioritize able-bodied people, but with those come prejudices and dominant attitudes that devalue people with disabilities. The idea of ablelism perpetuates a belief that assigns inferior value to people who have developmental, emotional, physical, or psychiatric disabilities.

Thin privilege: Like many privileges, thinness is an attribute that is societally desired, globally. Thin privilege is largely about visibility, because this specific body type is the one that is represented as the "standard" in all types of media. It is also about being seen as inherently more attractive and worthy of love. Thin privilege is about navigating the world without the constant dismissal of your body or the harassment faced by folks who don't fall into "thinness."

Fatphobia: Fatphobia is the misconception that bigger bodies are not beautiful, sexy, healthy, or desirable. We've all bought into the idea that beauty can only look a certain way, and one of the main attributes of beauty is thinness. Many of us have to unlearn how we

interact with fat bodies and how we seek to police them. We need to understand that our cultural obsession with dieting and losing weight is an expression of fear—a fear that if we get bigger, we are somehow "less."

White privilege: If we are to cover even broadly the various ways that bodies are judged and treated at a disadvantage, then race should be addressed. White privilege is a system that operates as the status quo, shaped by the position of power that white people have held economically and politically for centuries. White privilege does not mean that white people never experience disadvantages; however, in this system, people of color—who do not fit the "norms" of whiteness—are perceived as substandard in ways that range from subtle to truly dangerous, and, in many cases, lethal.

As we work through this journal, I want us to explore what it means when our bodies don't conform or won't conform. How can we validate them, regardless of what forces larger than us might be telling us about desirability or survival? That's the real work, right there. There are still so many things that I'm unfolding, unearthing, and exploring when it comes to my own human body. I know how hard it is to negotiate with yourself when you find that what stares out in front of you in the mirror doesn't fully encapsulate exactly who, or what, you are.

In that sense, I need this journal, too. I need a constant reminder that my body is mine alone. That there is nobody who has claim to it: no faith, no parent, no partner, no friend, and no definition of gender.

I alone have to navigate the ins and outs of what this body does, and therefore I have the choice to choose to be happy with it, despite the complications that I feel toward it every day. It's a process, and I'm learning to forgive myself for the self-hate that I carry. I'm learning to move on from the feeling of self-betrayal and accept that messy can also be a part of the journey.

My hope is that the more honest we are with our bodies and our own limitations, the more accepting we become of difference. As corny as it is, I believe in the power of liking yourself and that healing is perhaps the best journey we could ever be on.

"In a time when empowerment
is branded and sold to us in
millennial pink, self-love' is a
burden we are tasked with carrying.
It is a boulder we push eternally
up an incline. In short, it's work.
A lot of work. We are implored to
feel good about our bodies, our
relationships, the sex we have or
don't have. But the world around
us is not tasked with the same.
The structures that tell us we are
worthless if not thin, that we are
not desired, that our needs, comfort
and safety do not matter, remain
unmoved. You're not a bad feminist
or a bad person if you get tired of
trying to internalize a relentlessly
positive message at odds with
everything you've experienced in
your body. It's okay to put the
burden down and take a breath."

MUNA MIRE

It's important to accept the natural metamorphosis of our bodies, just as we accept that a butterfly can't return to its cocoon and that a snake can't go back into the skin it has shed. What if we are exactly where we're supposed to be in our bodies? What if we are constantly changing and in flux, but nonetheless exactly where we need to be? Think about what it would mean to embrace the journey of your body unfolding itself, as opposed to creating a rigid narrative for yourself and what your body should be.

YOU
CANNOT
GO BACK...
YOU CAN
ONLY GO
THROUGH...

Take a moment to write about the changes
that your body has gone through, focusing
on the ones that you felt resistant to.

Now write about the changes that you've come to appreciate or accept, and why.

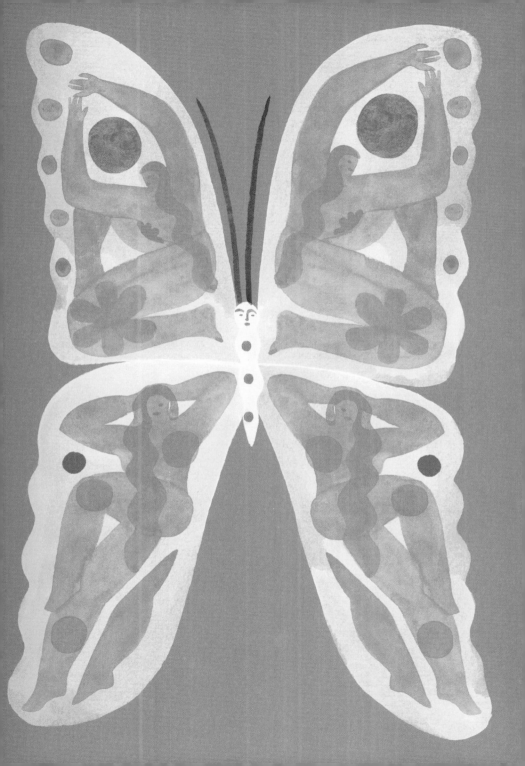

YOU ARE
YOURSELF
AT ANY SIZE...

Consider what Oprah once said in a promotion for Weight Watchers: "Inside every overweight woman is a woman she knows she can be." Statements like this perpetuate a myth that the "real" you is the smaller you, one that's buried inside the larger you. Even if you feel like your body doesn't represent you, which is a fair feeling, it is dangerous to attach the notion of your true self (the self that is worthy of love, opportunity, and good treatment) to one particular size. Your worthiness is not dismissible if you don't look the way you think you should look. You are the same person if you lose weight, as much as you are the same person when you put on weight.

Think about the relationship between your visible (physical) self and your invisible self (your personality, your character, your likes and dislikes). How do you envision it?

Make a true-you list.

List five things about yourself that have been
true through all phases of your life so far
(this can include anything—a personality quirk,
a color you love, or a conviction you've held).

1 _____

_____

_____

_____

_____

2 _____

_____

_____

_____

_____

3

4

5

Stop to reflect on all the specific and idiosyncratic things that make you proud of your body. Take a moment to take pride in your physical attributes, in your accomplishments, or even the unique beauty of your body type. These are all things that are specific to you and should be cherished. We are riveting beings in our uniqueness. There is no one else quite like us. All life's mysteries and circumstances made us into the beings we are. We are special, even if we don't feel that to be true every day, or ever. What are you proud of that's unique to you?

BEAUTY IS IN THE IDIOSYN-
CRASIES OF YOUR-
SELF.

Write about one of your favorite features.
What makes you appreciate it?

Keep a beauty list.
Make an ongoing list of things that you think are
beautiful about yourself, as you discover them.

"Girl, it's your body,
don't ever ever say you're sorry,
'cause you're not a copy."

VIVEK SHRAYA,
"GIRL IT'S YOUR TIME"

SCARS TELL A STORY. WHAT'S YOURS?

There are two types of scars: physical ones and emotional ones. Your physical scars are the marks of survival; how can we rewrite the idea that they are ugly or a source of shame? Emotional scars are the negative affirmations that seep into your nervous system, condense in your bloodstream, and become cellular. How do we begin to heal what we can't see? Start by paying attention to feelings like anger, insecurity, defensiveness, and numbness (or a desire to feel numb). Scar tissue is hard to break through, so take your time.

Tell the story behind one of your physical scars.

Write about an experience with your body that was emotionally scarring. Digest it by putting it onto the page, but only if it feels right. Sit with it, observing the feelings that come up.

We all have different limitations—there is just no denying it. None of us have the same physical abilities and talents, and it's important to remember that our limitations define us as much as our abilities do. Consider the idea that there is a positive side to acknowledging your limits. In doing so, you are forced to focus on and work with what you have. You might come to accept that what you once perceived as a limitation may actually be something that's a benefit to you and the direction of your life.

EACH BODY
HAS A
DIFFERENT
BANDWIDTH,
A DIFFERENT
PURPOSE,
A DIFFERENT
CAPABILITY.

It's important to be honest about the expectations of your body. Are you imposing any unrealistic expectations on yourself?

List your limits.
You can't be everything. You can only be yourself. List five things that you are *not*, with the understanding that acknowledging your limitations is one way of letting yourself be who you *are*.

1 _____

2 _____

3 _____

_____

_____

_____

_____

4 _____

_____

_____

_____

_____

5 _____

_____

_____

_____

_____

THERE IS NO WRONG WAY TO HAVE A BODY...

Remember that your body doesn't need to look beautiful or function "perfectly" (or even the way you think it should) to fulfill your purpose. It is hard to hold on to this very basic idea in a society that doesn't provide support for different bodies, especially ones that manage a chronic illness, an injury, or a disability. When you feel that your body is wrong, try to remember these feelings are not your fault. The root of the issue is that our society attempts to prioritize a specific kind of body. Bodies are complicated, but all bodies are valuable.

Take a moment to write honestly, without judgment, about how you're feeling about your body today. Do not attempt to iron out the contradictions.

_____

_____

_____

_____

_____

_____

_____

_____

_____

_____

_____

_____

_____

_____

_____

_____

_____

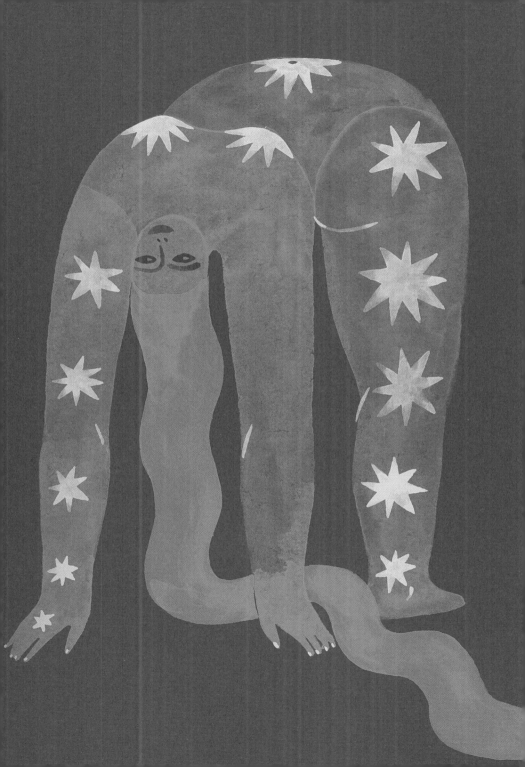

Make a curiosity list.
Take a moment to focus on the life of your mind and spirit and its pursuits. What do you want to read about, think about, and explore more deeply?

_____

_____

_____

_____

_____

_____

_____

_____

_____

_____

_____

_____

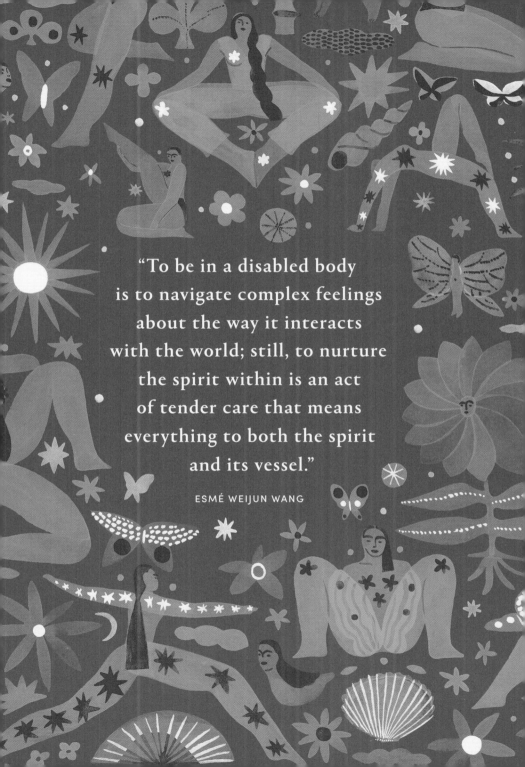

"To be in a disabled body
is to navigate complex feelings
about the way it interacts
with the world; still, to nurture
the spirit within is an act
of tender care that means
everything to both the spirit
and its vessel."

ESMÉ WEIJUN WANG

This is a moment for gratitude, particularly for the basic things your body does, its general strength, and the ways that your body facilitates and enables you to do things you enjoy. This doesn't look the same for everyone. You might want to focus your gratitude on the extraordinary things your body has bounced back from. At the very least (and most importantly), take a moment to appreciate your own willingness, despite how hard things can be at times, to keep going.

BE KIND
TO YOUR
BODY...
IT WORKS
SO HARD
FOR YOU
EVERY DAY...

Describe yourself, focusing not on what you lack, but on what you have. Be generous and specific, and use metaphors if you'd like. Compare yourself to no one.

List the happy moments.

Jot down five experiences, sensations,
or memories that make you happy that
you have a body.

1 _____
_____

_____

_____

2 _____
_____

_____

_____

3

4

5

"Learning to be at home
in your body, to be kind to it,
to let it breathe, to just let
it be is the biggest gift you can
give yourself. Come home
to it, take care of it; your body
is a beautiful thing . . .
just like you are."

NAOMI SHIMADA

BEAUTY IS A CON-
STRUCTED
IDEA. WHAT
WOULD
IT BE LIKE
TO REALLY
BELIEVE
THAT?

Beauty isn't real. In a lot of ways, it could be said that beauty is completely subjective. However, with the advent of capitalism, white privilege, and globalization, certain bodies have become what's seen as "the beauty must." In actuality, how many of us truly fit into the beauty ideal? It's important that we start unlearning certain markers we have stored in our minds about beauty, to truly accept and love ourselves wholly.

Think about the beauty standards that you have personally grappled with. When have you been most susceptible to them? What made you start to question them?

If you could invent a new beauty
ideal, what would it be?

It's that feeling that only one girl in the room can be the "prettiest." It is a faulty logic that this other woman is inherently attractive, and that you, when juxtaposed against her beauty, suddenly aren't. Can you think of stinging instances where a friend or someone else in your company received a compliment, and you felt diminished as a result? This is a product of being socialized to feel as though we're not enough. We are taught to dismantle other women, or else we dismantle ourselves.

ANOTHER
PERSON'S
BEAUTY
IS NOT AN
ABSENCE OF
YOUR OWN...

Think about someone you admire, love, or find beautiful. Do you see yourself as equally worthy? If so, what do you do to ensure that you give yourself that love first?

If not, what is in the way of seeing yourself as an equal?

Now compliment yourself
the way you would a friend.

WHY IS THINNESS A MAIN ATTRIBUTE OF BEAUTY?

We share so much common ground that thinness is ideal, that it's a worthy goal. Let's be clear: thinness as a natural body type should not be vilified. But as a society, we need to talk about thinness as a concept with transparency. Why is it assumed that we would all be happier and healthier and even more truly *ourselves* if we were thinner? Our culture connotes thinness with a certain brand of easy, carefree beauty, a chicness that is inherent, not calculated or primed to perfection. But in reality, the virtue of thinness is a construction *and* an imposition.

Letting go of the connection between thinness and happiness can be difficult, because it means abandoning a familiar and comfortable standard for selfhood. The process is known as "grieving the thin ideal." How do you relate to this concept?

Make a personal fulfillment list.
If you were to let go of this idea of selfhood
(thinner you = happier you), what other types
of fulfillment could you prioritize? List five here.

1

2

3

4

5

It's OK to take up space and feel good about yourself. In the patriarchy, femmes are discouraged from this because physical smallness and femininity have been stitched together to ensure that we don't take up *too* much space—or *more space* than we require. We have been contained so that we've begun to believe that our smallness is one of our most valuable qualities. What if more of us refused to be small or to be contained?

REFUSE TO MAKE YOURSELF SMALL.

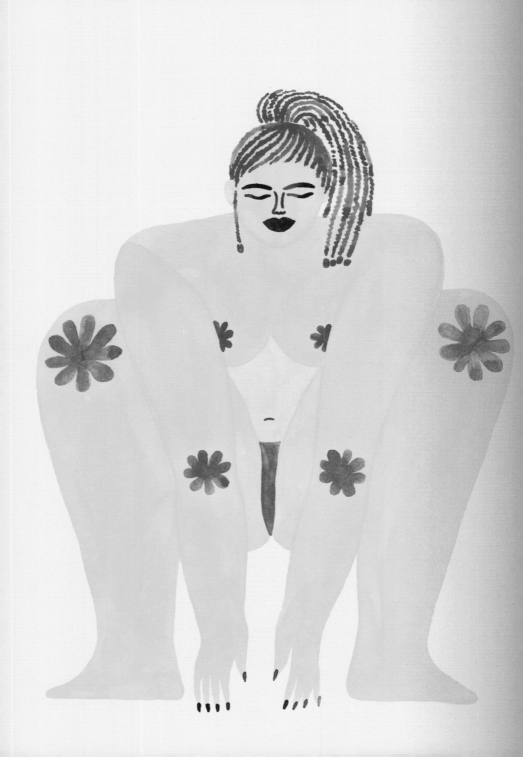

When you hear the phrase "It's OK
to take up space," how does it speak to
you and reassure you, specifically?

Create a confidence list.
Write down five things that you can
do to reinforce your self-confidence.

1 _____

2 _____

3

4

5

UNLEARN THAT HAPPINESS CAN ONLY BE ATTAINED IN A PARTICULAR KIND OF BODY...

Lindy West has written about how often people want to give her "advice" about her fatness, because they have a difficult time comprehending that someone who is fat could be content that way. She wrote in the *Guardian*: "I am so sorry that it is so hard to have a body—that even if your body is 'good' you need to chase that little thrill of superiority to feel safe. But fat people do not exist as leverage for thin people's self-esteem. We simply exist, same as anyone." Fatphobia is a socially acceptable form of discrimination, because we still feel free to talk and think about fatness as if it were a bad thing. The truth is that we are uncomfortable with anyone who does not conform to the standards society has placed on us.

Take a minute to write about your experience
with or beliefs about fatness.

Make a list for change.
Write down five things that you can do to push back against fatphobia (either socially or even just in your own mind).

1 _____

2 _____

3

4

5

Loving yourself is not a precondition to receiving love from others. You deserve to *receive* love despite how you may feel about yourself at any given moment. We have not been taught that this is true. In many ways, a large number of us have been taught that we need to be the perfect iteration of ourselves to receive the love we crave, and that becomes the narrative that binds us. When we don't find love, we invoke this idea that we are unlovable because we aren't "perfect." But that's simply not true. You are lovable at every size.

YOU
DESERVE
LOVE
AT ANY
SIZE.

Do you genuinely believe that you deserve
love at any size? If your knee-jerk response
is "no," take a moment to ask yourself *why*.

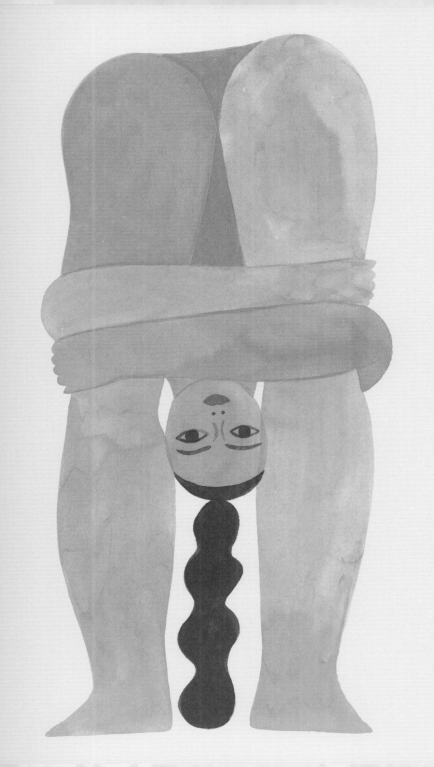

Make a loving list.

What do you do to offer yourself
encouragement, respect, and support?
Write down five ways that you can
treat yourself as you would a loved one.

1 _____

_____

_____

_____

2 _____

_____

_____

_____

3

4

5

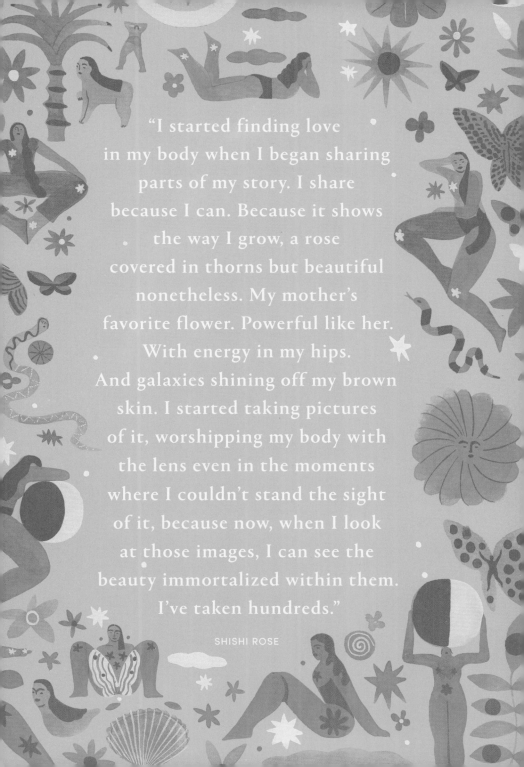

"I started finding love in my body when I began sharing parts of my story. I share because I can. Because it shows the way I grow, a rose covered in thorns but beautiful nonetheless. My mother's favorite flower. Powerful like her. With energy in my hips. And galaxies shining off my brown skin. I started taking pictures of it, worshipping my body with the lens even in the moments where I couldn't stand the sight of it, because now, when I look at those images, I can see the beauty immortalized within them. I've taken hundreds."

SHISHI ROSE

LISTEN TO THOSE WHO LOVE YOU.

It can be hard to see your own beauty, talents, and positive impact. You might lose sight of what the world would be missing without you, but your loved ones could readily tell you, if asked. So when you are having trouble seeing yourself, choose someone close and trusted and ask this person what they treasure in you. Be vulnerable and ask for vulnerability in return. It's OK to feel uncomfortable, but asking those who love you to reflect on what is great about you when you have a hard time remembering is an act of radical compassion.

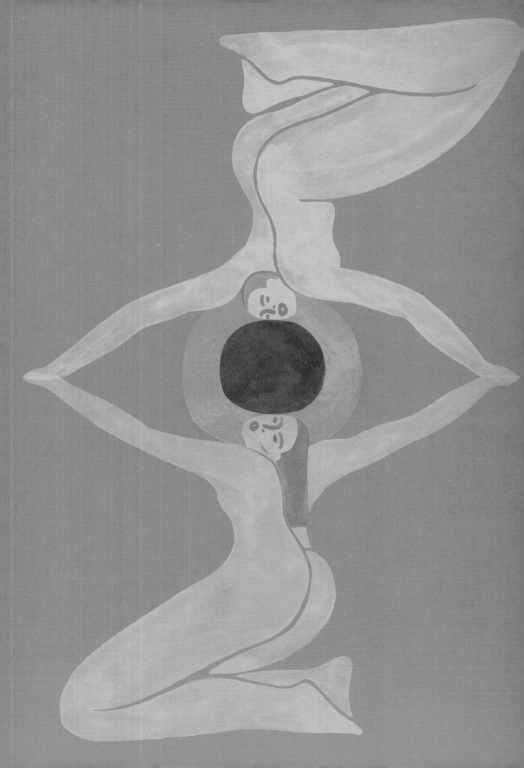

Initiate a conversation with someone close to you about what you value and admire most in each other. Record what you learned about yourself here. Any surprises?

Keep a compliments list.
Jot down positive feedback as you receive
it from others, giving yourself a chance
to savor their words. We need to learn to
hear compliments as loudly as we hear
the criticism in our own head.

We all have people in our lives who either unwittingly or intentionally undermine our self-confidence. Take a minute to think about those who chip away at your body-acceptance work. Consider their motives and consider whether this is a dynamic that can be discussed, or whether you need to set boundaries with this person. Do you need them in your life? It's OK to walk away from relationships that aren't serving you. Especially if they aren't uplifting you.

OTHER
PEOPLE'S
OPINIONS
DON'T
DETERMINE
YOUR
WORTH.

Write about an incident (could be a one-time thing or a recurrence) where an interaction with someone else made you feel physically inadequate.

Anticipate that this incident may happen
again and think about what you can say or
do in response. Even if it's just to yourself.

IN A SOCIETY THAT PROFITS FROM YOUR SELF-DOUBT, LIKING YOURSELF IS A REVOLUTIONARY ACT.

One of the simplest reasons that liking yourself is revolutionary is because countless industries thrive on the basic idea that we lack something or need to fix something about ourselves. It is also a result of living under capitalism, where the pursuit of "something better" is always on the horizon. We place liking ourselves in alternate realities and defer self-acceptance to a later date. So in a society like this one—in which we've been socially and culturally conditioned to accept a narrow definition of what is "normal" or "beautiful"—liking yourself is a radical act.

Make a toxic list.

Write down some of the culturally destructive messages about bodies that you experience through the media, commercial or public spaces, or on social media.

Pick the cultural message about bodies that
bothers you the most right now. Think about the
entities that stand to benefit from promoting this
message. Write a message of resistance here.

"You weren't born
in the wrong body.
You were born
in the wrong world."

ALOK VAID-MENON

Visit a spa, or simply sit in a public place and try to observe people without judgment. Go to an art museum and look at vastly different representations of the human form. Contemplate a variety of bodies in a way that feels comfortable for you. If social media triggers disparaging thoughts about bodies (yours or others), take a break. It's important in this process that there's no comparison, but an appreciation for the importance and worthiness of different kinds of bodies.

SEEK EXPOSURE TO ALL DIFFERENT BODIES.

Take any of the "field trips" suggested on the previous page and write about your experience below (what you did, what you remember).

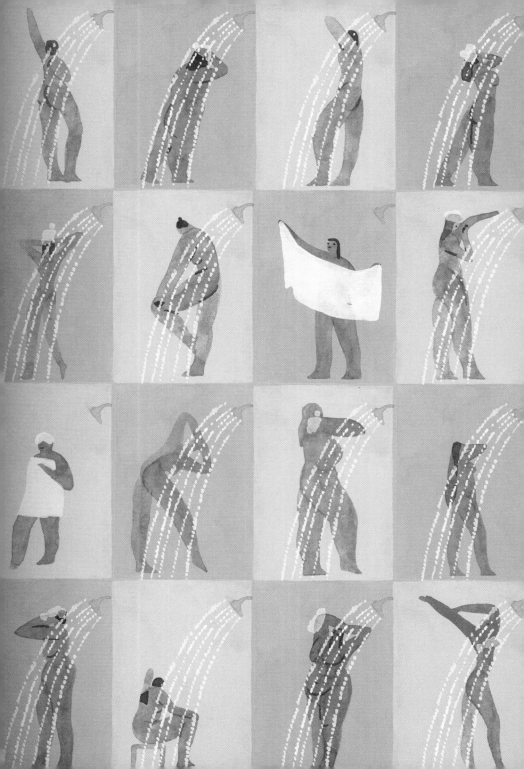

How does seeing a broader representation
of bodies affect the way you think about
your own body? Does it have an impact on
your concept of beauty?

ACCEPT
THE MESSINESS...
ACCEPT
THE MISTAKES...

It's OK if you don't feel good today. It's OK if you feel like you failed yourself. Self-love is not about being positive all the time. You must remember that even if you work really hard on self-acceptance, the process is not linear. Some days you might fall off the horse, and that's fine. There's no right answer when it comes to healing. Positivity is subjective, so don't push yourself toward an ideal that might be someone else's or even just impossible to maintain.

List your complaints.
Go ahead, get it off your chest.
What's bugging you at the moment?

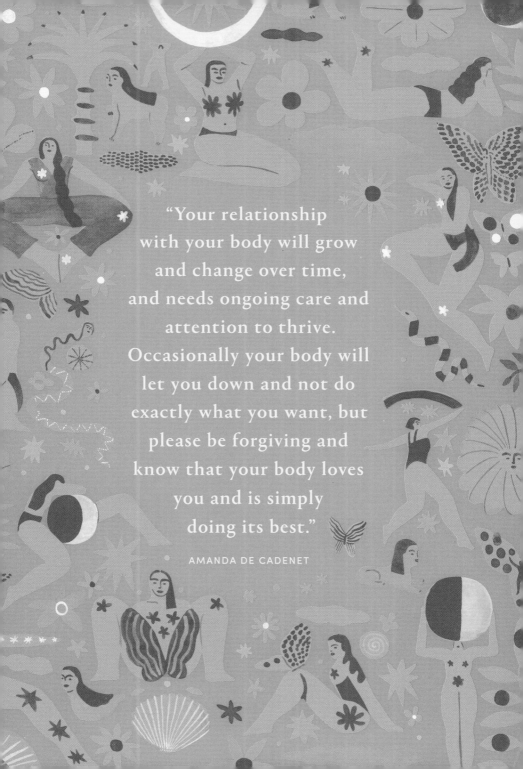

"Your relationship
with your body will grow
and change over time,
and needs ongoing care and
attention to thrive.
Occasionally your body will
let you down and not do
exactly what you want, but
please be forgiving and
know that your body loves
you and is simply
doing its best."

AMANDA DE CADENET

Life is too short to wait for approval to be the person you want to be. Your parents, family, or society might discourage you from being who you truly are, but the truth is you don't need them to give you permission. Giving *yourself* permission, however, is no easy feat. For example, you might think it is incentivizing to put off buying new clothes until *after* losing some weight. Ask yourself, honestly, if you are using this as an excuse to defer investing in yourself. Try saying, "I want to look good now! I want to wear clothes that I like now!" No more waiting for tomorrow to shine brighter.

DON'T WAIT
FOR A
BETTER TIME,
OR FOR
PERMISSION,
TO SHINE.

How do you shine? What does it mean
to be the best version of yourself?

Create a permission list.

Is there a fragrance, a hair dye, or a lipstick color you've been wanting to try? Or maybe a physical challenge or a new spiritual practice that you're curious about? Capture it all here.

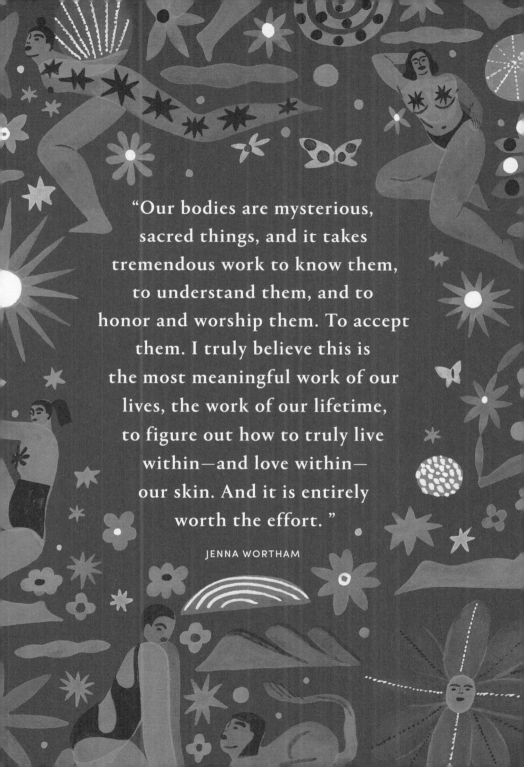

"Our bodies are mysterious, sacred things, and it takes tremendous work to know them, to understand them, and to honor and worship them. To accept them. I truly believe this is the most meaningful work of our lives, the work of our lifetime, to figure out how to truly live within—and love within—our skin. And it is entirely worth the effort."

JENNA WORTHAM

PRACTICE
MAKES
PRACTICE...

Accepting your body, healing your body, and loving your body is ongoing work and a source of endless learning, for as long as you have a body. Different strategies are needed for different times. You'll find one path, go down it, and encounter more ideas and practices that resonate with you. You may start practicing self-love and find fuel for wider activism. Practice doesn't make perfect. Practice leads to new and deeper ways of practicing.

Make a random realizations list.
Turn back to this page whenever you have a
body-positive breakthrough and jot it down here.